£2
go

Transforming the dinosaurs: how organisations learn

Sir Douglas Hague

Demos 1993

First published in 1993
by
Demos
120 Wilton Road
London SW1V 1GZ
Tel: 071 828 6231
Fax: 071 620 9271

Paper No. 3

ISBN 1 898309 10 8

Cover design by PENTAGRAM

Printed in Great Britain by
Gavin Martin
KGM House
26-34 Rothschild Street
West Norwood
London SE27 0HQ
Typesetting by Bailey Associates

Acknowledgements

I am very grateful to a group of people who took part in an evening discussion of my first thoughts for this paper. They challenged my ideas positively and helped me to formulate them more clearly and realistically. They were: Ian Hargreaves, Adele Blakeborough, Martin Jacques, Sir Peter Kemp, Charles Landry, Norman Strauss, Perri 6 and Bob Tyrrell.

I am also indebted to Norman Strauss for the learning we have shared on issues like these over the past decade, especially as joint founders of the Strategic Leadership Programme at Templeton College, Oxford. I thank him, not least, for his phrase 'cultural contagion.'

I am most grateful to Denise Edwards, as always, for her splendid secretarial speed and skill but now too for her ability to bear so patiently with my passion for exploiting the potential of computer technology by changing apparently finished manuscripts several times over.

An artist must never be a prisoner of himself, prisoner of a style, prisoner of a reputation, prisoner of success . . . Did not the Goncourt brothers write that Japanese artists of the great period changed their names several times during their lives? . . . They wanted to protect their freedom.

Matisse

1 INTRODUCTION

There is an anxiety across the land. During 1993 it began with sport and went deeper than British performance against the New Zealanders in rugby, the Australians in cricket and the world in soccer and tennis. The critics did not expect Britain to win all the races but they did expect us to be able to run them. The failure even to start the 1993 Grand National exposed the British racing authorities to ridicule, and appeared to symbolise a wider national failure.

Unhappiness, if not quite ridicule, then moved on to more august institutions. The current attack is concentrating on the Foreign Office, the Treasury and the Bank of England. The daily sight of Parliament on television raises doubts about whether the way it works and behaves is appropriate at the end of the 20th century. No institution is exempt. A recent television debate on a motion calling for 'fundamental change' in the British monarchy was defeated by a mere handful of votes in a total of over 250.

What is under attack is our national culture or, more precisely, the individual cultures of the institutions which make it up. This paper considers the fitness for the modern world of the cultures of British organisations, grand or common-place.

Its positive argument is that steps can be taken to change cultures for the better.

In the 1960s, the public image of British Gas made it the butt of national jokes - witness the success of the Flanders/Swann satirical song, 'The gas man cometh!' But recently, an opinion survey put British Gas second only to Marks and Spencer in public esteem. Of course, public image is not the same as actual performance, but given the amount of contact between employees of British

2

Gas and the public, the two cannot be widely different. British Gas has made an impressive change in its culture. Over the same period British Rail, whose public image in the 1960s was much better than that of British Gas, has come to occupy roughly the position previously held by British Gas.

In the 1980s, private-sector organisations' main concern was to respond to outside pressures. Competition and recession led managers to cut costs, to reduce labour forces and to keep inventories down. In the public-sector there was a similar emphasis, and innovations like the financial management initiative dominated thinking.

In the 1990s, by contrast, the primary task in both sectors must be to launch a cultural revolution.

2 CULTURES AND CHANGING THEM

Sociologists define the culture of an organisation as reflecting how those in it think and act as they carry out their tasks. It shows 'how we do things here.'[1]

An organisation's culture does not stand alone. To work, it must flow directly from values. If culture and values are not compatible those who work in the organisation may find it difficult to take their work seriously, since it will not fit with the values which the organisation pretends to espouse. Sooner or later, they will become disillusioned and resentful. They may even become mentally or physically ill.

It follows that the values and culture of any organisation, public or private, should be compatible. But as time moves on and the world changes, values will change and the culture will need to change too.

There are four main ways of achieving this:

a) Coercion

The first is coercion, the pressure exerted by competition or recession, which forces cultural change on businesses. Businesses are also coerced by threatened or actual take-over bids, or by strikes. All organisations are coerced by direct government interference in their affairs, and even more so by war, occupation by an enemy, or revolution.

b) Contagion

The second mechanism is contagion, which occurs when individuals or groups move in or are brought in, to enable an organisation to import the culture of the organisations from which they come. This is by no means easy. Action will be taken to contain or marginalise any newcomers: the British civil service talks of 'repelling boarders.' Alternatively the recipients may welcome the new arrivals, hoping that they will 'go native,' as the civil service puts it, and accept the local culture.

Individuals cannot achieve change on their own. Nor indeed can several newcomers if they come from different organisations, and do not share a common culture. Instead change depends on there being a coherent critical mass.[2] Take-overs are one way of providing this, so long as they bring a team which is sufficiently big, coherent or clever to reinforce its numbers and get its way.

c) Coaching

The third approach is coaching. When a sufficient number of an organisation's management team decides that the culture must be changed they may seek outside help. The organisation brings in experts to identify what changes in culture are needed and to find ways of achieving them. There is broad agreement among experts on organisational change about how this can be done although there is disagreement about the detail, as individual consultancies seek to promote their own approaches.

d) Learning

The fourth, and most desirable way of changing a culture is for the organisation to set about doing it for itself. This involves becoming, in today's vogue phrase, a learning organisation.[3] Few bodies in Britain have yet moved far in this direction, but it is what the future requires. An ability to innovate will be vital in a world of global competition, and learning is a key element in innovation (readers seeking a fuller understanding of organisational learning should consult the appendix).

Ideally every organisation in this country would become a learning organisation with its culture always evolving as its own future required. That is impossible: coercion, contagion and coaching will be needed too.

The next two sections of the paper therefore consider cultural issues in the private and the public sectors, identifying the kinds of change which are needed. The paper then goes on to propose remedies for the defects which are identified.

3 THE PRIVATE SECTOR

a) Positive Aspects

The private sector has many advantages in terms of cultural change. Market pressures mean that private sector organisations have no choice but to respond to shifts in the business environment, and especially in their markets, by changing their products, processes and policies. Whatever indicator of performance a business uses to track its performance, whether it be profit, share price or market share, failure to achieve its intended goals soon brings penalties, such as a crisis of cash flow or an inability to raise capital. Shareholders and financial experts in the media will put direct or indirect pressure on the organisation to improve performance if they judge it to be inadequate. Moreover there is also the external threat of takeover, which keeps potential victims on their toes.

Especially during periods like the recent recession, the ultimate penalty for not performing well enough is failure. Failure is a tough discipline, and not all victims of recession 'deserve' to fail. But an economy where no one failed would be less successful than ours, where some of the 'wrong' businesses fail, alongside the 'right' ones. Even if a business does fail, some at least of those who work for it will later find new jobs, painful although they may find the transition. Similarly, the more successful divisions in a firm which fails may be taken over or reconstructed and will continue to operate.

In the terminology we are using, change in the culture of private sector organisations may be slower than it would be if all private organisations could learn to change their own cultures or were coached to do so. Yet even for those which do not, in the end competition, take-over or outright failure bring change. The mills of God (or is it Mammon?) may grind slowly but they grind effectively in the end.

b) Some Concerns

Although the private sector tends to resist stagnation, I want to point to three concerns.

Monopoly Policy

The first is that an active government competition policy is the only guarantee that competition remains adequate. In the UK this means relying on the Office of Fair Trading to identify potential problem areas, on the Monopolies and Mergers Commission to investigate them imaginatively and on the Department of Trade and Industry to act wisely on these recommendations.

For as far ahead as one can see the strength of global competition, linked to technological change, will act as a powerful force for change. But it will still need reinforcement through an effective competition policy. The present arrangements give great power to the President of the Board of Trade who can, if he wishes, reject recommendations from the Monopolies and Mergers Commission without giving reasons. There is similar concern that only the Office of Fair Trading can ask for an investigation by the Commission. As in Germany, competition policy should be strengthened by giving members of the public the right to call for investigations.

Top Peoples' Pay

The second concern is more immediate. It is worrying because it suggests a defect in the top management culture of many companies. Since 1989, there has been a growing divergence between movements in company profits and changes in top-executive pay. Profits have fallen, but top executive pay has risen, on average, not merely faster than retail prices but faster than the pay of any other group. Resigning and retiring executives have received huge pay-offs, giving the impression that the financial reward a top executive receives, while theoretically linked to performance, can be greater in the case of failure than success. Comment is concentrated especially on BP, Invesco, Lasmo and Trafalgar House. Some senior executives (two-thirds of top chairmen and chief executives according to one survey in 1992) have had three-year rolling contracts - in other words, 36 months' notice of dismissal! The appointment of stronger independent non-executive directors to settle directors pay is being proposed as a solution, but their attitudes and culture may not prevail if these are at odds with the remainder of the Board.

Corporate Governance

The recent debate about corporate governance has emphasised the insufficient oversight and engagement of major investors. This lack of external discipline has allowed some firms to act irresponsibly or even illegally. It has also blunted the external pressures for change. But there is also now an opposite danger. The threat is that the failure of what even Sir Adrian Cadbury has described as a 'last chance for self-regulation' will lead to the imposition of excessive bureaucratic requirements which will divert businesses from their core functions.[4]

Inertia at the top?

Fourth, concern is often expressed over whether people at the top of private sector organisations move to new jobs soon enough. Amongst the top industrial and financial businesses in the UK, one finds that Lord Weinstock has been Managing Director of GEC for 30 years; Lord Hanson has been Chairman of Hanson for 28 years; D C Bonham Chief Executive of Hanson for 29 years; Ernest Harrison, Chairman of Racal for 27 years; Sir John Clark, Chief Executive Officer of Plessey for 27 years; Cyril Stern chairman of Ladbrookes for 22 years; Sir Edward Nixon, Managing Director or Chief Executive Officer of IBM for 21 years; Sir Peter Walters, Managing

Director of BP for 17 years; Sir Jeremy Morse, Chairman of Lloyds Bank for 16 years; Sir Adrian Cadbury, Chairman of Cadbury for 14 years; and Sir James Ball, Chairman of Legal and General for 13 years. If one looks simply at directorships - executive or non-executive - the number of people serving for more than 20 years on a particular board is large.

These figures may be misleading for the future. Most of those listed have now left their companies and the present holders of the posts of chairman and chief executive have been there, on average, for about three and a half years.[5] Some companies, such as ICI, have always changed their chairmanship much more frequently. The four predecessors of Sir Denys Henderson, who has himself been Chairman for 6 years, served for an average of 4 years. But in the top 50 companies, even now, four top executives have already served for more than 15 years and five for more than 10.

4 THE PUBLIC SECTOR

By comparison with the private sector, the public sector appears stable, even sedate. It is certainly more homogeneous, but in some respects it is more complex. Running a private business can be rather easy compared with operating in the public sector.

The first reason may appear paradoxical. A modern business deals with great complexity. This arises from its technology, products, processes, people, and internal control systems. It is exacerbated by the external constraints imposed by competition, legislation, and the rules and procedures of the stock exchange. Yet this very complexity drives those who manage businesses to find devices for making the process of management tolerable and they do so by heroic simplification.

They reduce the huge complexity of the business to a relatively small number of figures - often financial - in its management accounts and other documents. To be sure, the documents may themselves be complex but they are nevertheless simple compared with the complexity they are reflecting. In extreme cases - but far from unusual ones - a management will simplify its task by concentrating on equating changes in performance with changes in profit. This attitude is supported by reports in the media which frequently reduce the complex variety of a huge multi-national business to a single profit figure - the ultimate variety reduction.[6] They do not manage complex systems, they avoid admitting that they are complex. The more they 'manage by the numbers,' the more the moral dilemmas and intellectual conundrums which management could - perhaps should - face are concealed or avoided.

The second simplicity open to a private business is that it can define its purpose and objectives for itself in the light of its values. If part of the company becomes too unimportant or too burdensome for non-financial reasons, it can be closed down or sold. More frequently, a unit or subsidiary will be closed because it is losing money and because, were losses to continue, the future of the whole business would be threatened. The media and the public may agonise about jobs lost and markets sacrificed: there may well be agonising within the business. But the company can insist that its decision is acceptable because, in the end, it is compatible with its values.

I am, of course, over-simplifying; not all companies define their objectives so narrowly. But I am not dramatically over-simplifying. Moreover, the role and objectives of a private company are established by some combination of its top management and board - occasionally with its employees. They are not established for it by legislation or government instruction.

¹ Can change its own prices
² Customers determine quality value for money

The three big differences between the public and private sectors are therefore these. First, the role of a public sector organisation is defined for it, however generally, from outside, so that its objectives will almost always be broader than those of a profit-oriented private sector entity. Among other things, this means that it is harder to 'bend the rules,' and that more people must be involved in, and told about, decisions. There is a consequent slowness or reluctance to change, sometimes even to act.

The second big difference is that it is almost always more difficult for a public sector organisation to abandon activities than it is for a private business. Schools cannot decide to stop educating five year olds. The health service cannot refuse to treat patients in Sussex. Yet a private company can easily withdraw from markets, or reduce its product range.

The third difference is both surprising and very positive. By comparison with the private sector, top civil servants are moved much more frequently and deliberately. This is a clear benefit from the fact that the civil service is monolithic. Movement can be planned and enforced centrally. Sir Robert (now Lord) Armstrong was Secretary to the Cabinet for 8 years; Sir Peter Middleton was Head of the Treasury for 8 years and Sir Douglas Wass for 9. The three predecessors of the present Permanent Secretary of the Department for Education served for an average of about 5 years. One can, however, worry that so few of the leading mandarins move outside the public sector during their careers, although many do after they retire. Moreover, as one moves from the centre of government, periods in post become longer. Sir Claus Moser was Head of the Central Statistical Office for 11 years; Sir John Mason, Director General of the Meteorological Office for 18 years and Sir Adrian Cadbury has been a Director of the Bank of England for 23 years.

a) Education

The remainder of this section considers the cultures of education, the civil service and government agencies in that order, focusing in particular on their capacity to encourage learning.

Figure 1 provides a useful tool for studying educational institutions. These must, after all, have a primary responsibility for promoting a learning culture. The vertical axis shows the components of education, the horizontal axis the means of learning. It draws on important and refreshing work by Howard Gardner, Professor of Education at the Harvard Graduate School, not least his book *Frames of Mind*.[7]

As in the USA, we in this country are instilled with the belief that the prime aim of education is to give us what Gardner calls logical-mathematical skills. Linguistic understanding is also given, but all too often without the ability actually to speak a foreign language at all well. The acquisition of interpersonal skills is largely ignored. Spatial skills - like sailing or hunting - are important in primitive societies, and their modern equivalents can be found in construction, manufacturing and driving today. Finally, bodily skills may be acquired, such as dancing, acting and sports.

Along the top axis are shown the ways in which education is carried out. These begin with 'chalk and talk,' the reading of books and the use of information and communications technology. All are largely concerned with logical-mathematical learning. Only with discussion and teamwork is there much acquisition of interpersonal skills. One also learns from work itself. Finally, one can learn by watching what someone else does in his or her job.

FIGURE 1

EDUCATIONAL COMPONENTS	METHOD OF TRANSMISSION						
	Chalk and Talk	Reading	Audio-Visual	Discussion	Team Activity	Learn by Watching	Work
Logical-Mathematical							
Linguistic							
Interpersonal							
Bodily-PE/Sport							
Work Skills							

The matrix provides a helpful way for schools, universities, employers and others to consider whether a particular institution or course gives a broad enough spread of types of discipline and methods of learning. At present almost all of them use too few learning methods, even if they offer enough fields of study. We should expect education and training bodies not only to cover a substantial number of the cells in the matrix, but also to be able to give a coherent justification for those which they choose.

i) Schools

All available evidence suggests that the cultures of the state schools - and of the civil servants who oversee them - put too little emphasis on learning as opposed to teaching. To develop successful 'learning organisations' those who work in them must know how to learn and how to pass that knowledge on. The education system should therefore be working hard to wean students away from reliance on teachers and towards books and electronic data-bases. That this is not happening in the UK is indicated by the fact that staffing per student is higher in secondary schools than at the primary and pre-primary level. Chalk and talk still play too big a part. Schools are too concerned with the top left-hand corner of Figure 1, and that in three senses.

First, they do not emphasise the need to learn how to learn.

Second, there is too little overlap between schools and the world outside. Even within schools, there are two overlapping cultures - a professional, educational culture and a public sector one. Together they mean that too many teachers are cut off from the world in which their students will work and live. Yet teachers hold that it is they who know what should be taught, not parents, the

Secretary of State for Education or employers. The problem is that most teachers' views of future skills needs rest on second- or third-hand interpretations of what work currently requires of school leavers, when what is actually required is an understanding of the skills which work and life will demand of teenagers towards the end of the 1990s.

Third, schools do not devote enough time and energy to enabling students to work as members of learning teams. Rather oddly, this is increasingly the case as children grow older. By contrast, recruiters from business take a great interest in the extent to which school children and graduates have played team games. They treat it as a proxy for the ability to work in learning teams.

In tackling these problems the contribution of the civil servants in the Department for Education has not been good enough. There is general agreement that a National Curriculum is needed, although the argument over whether it is forward-looking and broad enough has not been resolved. But when it comes to implementation the Department has assumed that teachers will accept an amount of outside direction and form-filling which only a civil servant could have thought appropriate.

There are, however, also much deeper issues. Educational policy has rightly grasped that British children need to be as well-educated, and in the same fields, as German and Japanese children if they are to compete with them in world markets. What is not clear is whether the Department for Education has moved beyond trying to replicate in Britain what seemed appropriate in Germany in the 1960s. Some schools seeking computer systems have been pressed to take numerically-controlled machine tools instead, on the grounds that that is what the Germans would have offered. What will actually be required is a much broader ability to think and to learn in the highly-computerised world of the next millennium. If German education really is stuck in the 1960s that can only be good for Britain; there is no need to emulate it!

The general conclusion must be that despite splendid exceptions, British schools are still not moving rapidly and confidently enough into using information technology. British secondary schools appear to spend more than 80% of their total budget on teachers[8] Yet this is a time when at least some of what teachers do needs to be replaced by information and communications technology if schools are to keep up with the rest of the economy in terms of effectiveness as well as productivity.

But the problem goes deeper still. After a hundred years or so of compulsory formal education, schools are still failing to provide the school leavers we need. As one educator has suggested, perhaps the current system and the assumptions which underlie it have now become part of the problem, not the solution.

A similar point has been well made by Howard Gardner. His book, *The Unschooled Mind*, points to an alarming transition faced by children when they start school. He writes that 'somehow the natural or intuitive learning that takes place in one's home or immediate surroundings during the first years of life seems of an entirely different order from the school learning that is now required throughout the literate world.' He goes on to argue that 'those of us in education have not appreciated the strength of the initial conceptions [and] stereotypes . . . that students bring to their learning nor the difficulty of refashioning or eradicating them. We have failed to appreciate that in nearly every student there is a five-year-old 'unschooled' mind struggling to get out and express itself.'[9]

Educators therefore need to exploit the innate powers of the infant mind, to recognize the difficulties which schoolchildren have in learning particular disciplines - not least mathematics - and, on this basis, to restructure the whole school system. Gardner argues that reform depends on working equally upon four different levels: assessment, curriculum, teacher education and community support. He implies that British educational policy is homing in on some of the right issues but in far too uninformed a way, and that our educational culture has not caught up with the modern world.

Enough has been said to show that we face serious problems with the overlapping cultures of teachers and civil servants - not to mention politicians. All these cultures need radical change if our schools are to provide what we require of them in the 21st century.

ii) Universities

Perhaps surprisingly, in view of the accumulated brain power within them, the situation in British universities is if anything worse than in schools. There are five particularly striking failings.

First, even in the late 20th century, they remain too cut off from the world outside - especially business and their local communities. This criticism is less deserved by polytechnics, which have recently been granted the status of universities, but there is room for improvement there too. The isolation of universities is based partly on a reluctance, bred of supposedly superior intellect, to become involved in the grubby realities outside, especially in the commercial world. Simultaneously they also have the opposite fear that in the commercial world this intellect would be scorned for its inability to cope.

Second, universities are more backward in their use of information technology than schools. Yet even more than schools, universities will in future have to use modern communications technology - films, audio-and-video material on compact discs, and television (especially closed-circuit television).[10] Very few universities have grasped what these technologies will demand of them in the 21st century. Even fewer have begun to move in that direction, although the Open University is a splendid exception. Instead, universities concentrate narrowly on the top left-hand corner of Figure 1.

Third, virtually everyone in a university refers to what they do as 'teaching.' Hardly anyone, outside a Psychology Department, talks of learning. Yet the ability to learn is what the outside world, and therefore the educational system, should prize above all.

Fourth, universities largely ignore their peers and alumni who have become specialists outside academia. Part of the reason is that it is logistically difficult to keep growing numbers of graduates up to date professionally and personally. Yet it is also a tremendous opportunity. Follow-through and refresher programmes could be a huge source of income and interest. Part of the reluctance to work with alumni again springs from fear. Graduates returning for more education would not be satisfied with the rather out-of-date material and sloppy presentation of the typical academic.

Fifth, there are problems over research. The main difficulty is that virtually everyone who works in a university derives his or her view of how research should be organised from the picture of an idealised, archetypal university where everyone is a scholar, engaged equally both in teaching and research. The academic community is reluctant to allow some individuals or universities to specialise on research, leaving others to specialise in what are seen as less prestigious activities, especially teaching. Teaching carries such low esteem that only a few brave (or stupid?) souls see it as the sole basis for a career.

The result is that too much research is not up to scratch, whether it is carried out by academics in the time they do not devote to teaching and preparation, or financed by outside bodies like the government-funded Research Councils. Thus far, no one has had the courage to act toughly, although the Higher Education Funding Council for England (HEFCE) is creeping up on the problem.

Oddly, the high prestige given to research is not matched by a willingness to share its findings. Even when it is of great interest to non-academics, research findings are too rarely presented in a form and in publications which those in the 'real world' will read. Yet, having been reluctant to the point of obduracy about making their research generally available, some academics are apoplectic about letting good journalists do it for them.

Peter Drucker has rightly said that 'there is a terrible post-war fallacy that if more than three people in the world understand what you are saying, then you are not a serious scholar.'[11] and that 'obscurantism' has even 'infected business schools'. If this is true of business schools which are intended to be practical, it is even more true of universities. The curse of American business schools, and of many, although not all, British ones, is the belief that only US-style PhD programmes can produce competent business school teachers. The presumption is that the best preparation for becoming a teacher of business is to spend two or three years in difficult academic research, applying principles and techniques developed by a profession whose main aim seems to be to make what it learns inaccessible to people in business.

Research findings are kept within a small, closed community of peers and are, so far as the outside world is concerned, often 'wasted.' This is not so true in science and medicine although, even there, it is probably more true than its practitioners would accept. Certainly in the social sciences, whose role should surely be to reflect the realities of society back to us, university research is too theoretical, too conceptual, and too remote.

The civil service contribution to universities has not been very helpful. Partly because it was traditionally seen as necessary to preserve the 'independence' of state-funded universities and partly because it is a way to draw on specialist knowledge in the universities which the civil service does not possess, funding for and supervision of universities is carried out by the Higher Education Funding Council for England (HEFCE). Within it, existing cultures continue. Academics bring in the university culture; civil servants bring in theirs; and business frets because their managerial culture finds little resonance in either of the other two.

The HEFCE has continued its predecessor's policy, begun in the late 1980s, of gradually channelling funds towards the more highly-rated universities. This has two defects.

First, in assessing a university, the HEFCE relies on the judgements of academic peers who act as assessors and referees within an in-bred system. This is a neo-Stalinist approach. It is based on the assumption that (with the help of peer groups of academics) the Council can evaluate teaching, and especially research, in every university. The method virtually guarantees that more research publications are seen as better than fewer, provided that they appear in journals 'refereed' by members of a closed group of peers, and it means that quantity acts too often as a proxy for quality. The method also suffers from the defects of any culture which assumes that 'if you can't measure it, it doesn't exist.'

Lying behind all of these issues is a very unfashionable question. The conventional argument for increasing the proportion of young people being given an academic training, with its related examinations, is that this will stop our relative economic decline, or even reverse it. This argument is far from self-evident. The point was, as Michael Dixon says, 'glossed over by the committee of inquiry headed by the late Lord Robbins which in 1963 recommended the first post-war expansion of higher education. No one seriously challenged the belief that more young people educated to what universities considered to be a higher level would somehow make the nation more productive as well as civilised'.[12]

Since a university training was never intended as a training for a real-world job, it will only succeed in this by chance, not design. Even at this late stage, it would be sensible to convert at least half our universities into polytechnics, concerned with professional training in fields such as science, engineering and business.

b) The Civil Service

The civil service is at its best when establishing procedures, setting rules and applying these, on the whole rigorously, to high-volume and rather routine activities, like the payment of social security benefits. Such routine processing activities - for example, the issuing of driving and vehicle licences - are now being hived off to relatively independent organisations. They are still part of the civil service and therefore part of government but some of them will probably soon be privatised. The vehicle testing centres may well be the first.

Policy and supervisory work

While these functions are being devolved, the core civil service is now being asked to concentrate on policy work and the supervision of agencies. To do that well will call for a substantial change in how the civil service thinks and operates.[13]

Many civil servants will deny this. But they will do so mainly because they under-rate their own deficiencies in tackling issues of strategy and policy. In my view there are three particularly important weaknesses.

First, the traditional qualities instilled into civil servants by their training and reinforced by the civil service culture are inappropriate for policy work. This requires vision, imagination and innovation, not obedience to rules established by others and careful attendance to detail.

Second, the civil service culture is predominantly literary. The best civil servants write well, but even the best writing is not always sufficient. To make sense of the complex socio-technical systems of the modern world requires theory and analysis to match. Mathematics, statistics and diagrams are essential.[14]

This leads to the third failing. Such modes of thought give much the best results if used by groups, not individuals. Groups can best argue over their equations and even more their diagrams if they use such things as flipcharts and whiteboards. Indeed, some argue that the test today of how far someone is a leading edge thinker is how long it takes him or her to jump to the whiteboard to show an equation or a diagram to others in the group.

That Whitehall is not comfortable with visual aids is illustrated by a revealing incident. When Sir John Hoskyns became head of the Policy Unit at Downing Street in 1979, he installed a flipchart in his office which was heavily used in analysing and debating the strategic issues facing the UK. When Sir John left the Policy Unit, the flipchart was immediately stored away in a corridor. After a couple of weeks, it disappeared altogether.

As this implies, civil service thinking and policy making is too often a solitary process. Yet, given the complexity of the world, one person's brain, however outstanding, can no longer hope to analyse it well. To do so would require so large an investment of time in learning a range of academic and other disciplines that it is no longer practicable.

The analytical and policy work on which the central civil service will now concentrate therefore requires not individuals but multi-disciplinary teams, whose members between them have good scientific, technological, economic, social and managerial knowledge, together with intellectual and practical experience. The apparent failure of the civil service even to comprehend the issues which this raises, let alone to construct and use effective teams, represents its most serious failing.[15]

When challenged, any mandarin will assure you that strenuous efforts are being made to improve civil service management. My own experience, for example with the financial management initiative, is that the Whitehall culture is unable to do more than convert interesting managerial ideas into arid essays or boring check lists.

Some perceptive civil servants would argue that there is an even bigger gap. Sir Peter Kemp, a former permanent secretary for the civil service believes that it lies between the policy makers and those responsible for implementation. The civil service lacks what he calls project managers who, told what a new policy is, will say, 'this is how to implement it,' or even, 'this cannot be done.'

c) Government Agencies

The biggest structural change in the civil service for many years, perhaps ever, has been the conversion of a substantial part of the service into a range of quasi-governmental agencies, currently about 90 in total, and generally known as the next steps agencies after the 1988 report to the Prime Minister, entitled *Improving Management in Government: The Next Steps.*[16]

They employ their own staffs, who need not be Crown servants. With a clear division of responsibilities between the Chairman or Chief Executive of each agency and the Minister or Permanent Secretary to whom they report, the role of the agency is to concentrate on providing its own service or product. It is required to improve delivery while also increasing efficiency.

The important point for the argument being developed here is that while the tasks which the agencies perform will not, at least initially, be different from those they engaged in as part of the civil service, they are to have 'as much independence as possible,' with increasing freedom 'to recruit, pay, grade and structure' themselves, within a framework of accountability to their parent departments. Many agencies, of course, will have large numbers of local offices and the intention is to give suitable autonomy to their managements as well as to the agency as a whole.

If the new system is to work well, agencies will have to create their own cultures. This is recognised at the very beginning of the report, which states that success 'depends heavily on changing the cultural attitudes and behaviour of government.' It rightly insists that to ensure that departments have people with the managerial skills needed to run agencies, relatively junior members of departments must be given 'substantial experience of the skills and practical reality of management.' It goes on to point to the need for training, secondment to other organisations and some early promotions.

But the report leaves one wary about the likelihood of

cultural change. The services which agencies are to provide are defined for them in advance, leaving them little freedom to decide what their clients really want.

Contrary to Howard Gardner's ideas there is also a clear implication in 'Next Steps' that experience alone, with no carefully tailored link to other forms of training, is preferable to training courses - as although the two can never be helpfully linked. Conversations with senior civil servants suggest that they have lost faith in formal training courses after their large scale use in the 1980s failed to bring about the hoped for change in culture and behaviour. This may explain today's faith in training on the job. What would be preferable is an approach to training and learning which comes from both the top left-hand and the bottom right-hand corners of Figure 1 (and perhaps the centre, as well, at least in terms of learning methods).

The Next Steps report is written in conformity with the civil service's literary tradition. Even within that, the word 'learning' never appears. It is a document written by people who realise that the key task is to change the civil service culture but who manifestly do not have a feel for the management of change 'in their bones.'

d) How can Cultures Change?

Figure 2 shows how far the sources of cultural change which we have identified (coercion, contagion, coaching and learning) have an impact in the private and public sectors. It shows that coercion and contagion have at least a moderate impact in changing culture in the private sector, although the effect of coaching and learning is problematical, and almost certainly smaller. In the public sector, coercion, contagion and learning appear to have little effect. The influence of coaching is virtually unknown.

FIGURE 2

SOURCE OF CHANGE	PRIVATE SECTOR	PUBLIC SECTOR
COERCION	MODERATE TO HIGH	LOW
CONTAGION	MODERATE TO HIGH	LOW
COACHING	?	?
LEARNING	?	LOW

On this basis, we look in Sections 5 and 6 at ways in which the situation revealed in Figure 2 might be improved.

5 ISSUES FOR PEOPLE

a) How long in a job?

Top executives

Since we are concerned with changing organisational culture, our main concern must be with the top of each organisation, where its tone is set. We have seen that the issue of whether individuals stay in the same job is mainly one for the private sector, especially now that change in the technological, economic and social environment of business is so rapid. Those who lead organisations need to be fresh and imaginative. This is difficult after more than a decade in the same job. Nothing can guarantee freshness and imagination, but the one thing that will almost guarantee the opposite is for those in the top two or three tiers of management to remain there for long periods. If they do, they become habituated to the way the organisation operates. They lose their acuteness in observing what is going on both within the organisation and outside it, and, perhaps, in their judgements of people and decisions.

I therefore advocate that no one in these top tiers should remain in the same job for more than five years. I emphasise that this should apply to all jobs, public or private, because while those in the very top civil service jobs move regularly, this does not always happen in more peripheral agencies or in the jobs immediately below the top in national and local government.

Well before the end of his or her first year, the newcomer to any job will have had time to work out what changes are needed. A further year will normally be adequate for making them. A further two years will give time for the changes to be absorbed and for the organisation to return to operating on an even keel. At the end of five years, the incumbent should be ready to move on.

Making all possible allowances - for example, for outstanding performance in a particular job - one might give an outside limit of seven years, but this is probably over-generous. We should become used to these as rigid limits in major organisations, public or private.

Even in entrepreneurial businesses people need to move on, devastating although this may seem to the typical entrepreneur. There is a barrier through which the entrepreneurial firm must pass if it is to become substantial. Some say that this is when the entrepreneur no longer interacts with all employees. I would myself put it at a turnover of £3 million to £4 million per annum. To move beyond this, the founding entrepreneur, or entrepreneurial team, may have to surrender control. What is more, even if this first barrier is passed, there are others to come.

Where a business with a turnover of less than, say, £10 million is taken over, the acquirer should do so on the basis that the existing management team will have to be replaced *in toto*. The common practice of inducing management teams to remain, through the offer of 'earn-outs' which offer them substantial payments if predetermined profits are achieved in the next few years, is often a mistake.

Non-executives

Similar rules should apply to non-executive directors both of private companies and on public boards. I advocate an initial appointment of two years, followed by further appointments of not more than two years each, up to a maximum of six years. After that, the same person should never again be a non-executive member of the same board.

It is more difficult to construct general rules to apply lower down an organisation, although similar ones should apply at the top of major subsidiaries of large companies. Nevertheless, the application of these rules at the top would create an attitude towards change which would lead to more movement lower down.

Specialists

There are, however, other issues. In particular, how should specialists, as opposed to generalist managers or administrators, be treated? Strong opposition to the notion of time-limited jobs would undoubtedly come from specialists, not least from scientists and other academics as well as from professionals such as accountants and lawyers. One can assert this with confidence for scientists and academics, since many already resist suggestions that they should move into management jobs, even as leaders of laboratories or university departments, where such a move is part of an established career progression.

But it is far from clear that even a dedicated specialist, who resists all pressure for a career move and remains working for a lifetime in a narrow professional field, benefits much in the end. Nor is it clear that the world outside benefits from overspecialisation.

This issue has two aspects. First, I would not go as far as the eminent British scientist Sir John Mason, already mentioned. He insists that 'anyone can become a world expert in anything in two years.' Yet I would still argue strongly that new intellectual fields are easier to enter and understand than experts within them contend.

Second, and more important, after years working in the same field it is harder than most experts recognise to keep a mind which is so genuinely exploring and inquisitive that it can reopen issues long seen as settled[7]

A newcomer to a specialist field is more likely than established practitioners to ask the naive or unconventional question, or to notice the previously unrecognised patterns which lead to advance. The contribution of Crick and Watson to the discovery of the double helix and thus to the current revolution in genetics is only one outstanding example. [18]

Crick, then in his mid-30s, was being pressed by his superiors to complete a PhD on a topic unrelated to the helix. Both Crick and Watson were told that Sir Laurence Bragg, head of the Cavendish Laboratory, where they were working, insisted that they should 'give up DNA.' He did so without compunction because experts he consulted had told him that there was nothing original in their approach. Fortunately for them, they found ways of ignoring Bragg's instruction.

Much of today's scientific advance is taking place across the boundaries of long-established academic disciplines. This is leading to demarcation disputes as fierce as any in industry. Non-scientists noted with wry amusement that to physicists the crime of those who claimed to have discovered 'cold fusion' was not that they were wrong. It was that, even had they been right, as chemists they had no business to be working in that field at all. Similarly, government funding of important new biological research in the UK was held up during the 1980s by a fierce dispute between the Agriculture and Food, Medical, and Science and Engineering Research Councils about who had legitimate rights over this research field.

If, as I believe, lack of innovation in research - scientific and other - is one element in the British malaise, we need freer movement between specialist fields. This is as true in professional fields in industry and commerce as in academic ones. I see no reason to exempt specialists from the kind of job and career moves I am advocating.

The blight of over-specialisation

In practice, the real world has to do what it can to offset the excessive specialisation of the educational system. As Peter Hennessy has commented, this is 'now a blight at pretty well every level.' It 'leaves professionals unable to talk to each other, ever prone to caricature and dismissing what they don't understand.'[19] Since the educational system is unwilling to change this, it is up to the rest of us to do so. The development of a culture in which both specialists and generalists move more freely between jobs can only be beneficial for Britain.

But the universities also need to rise to a challenge as severe as any posed to schools by Howard Gardner. We need somehow to produce graduates who can think laterally, and who can think about thinking - and learning. Perhaps universities should primarily offer a kind of meta-thinking into which all specialisms can fit.

b) How long in an organisation?

Moving around the company

Even conceptually, this issue is trickier than it looks. Obviously, if we could reach a situation where the individuals who lead and set the tone of all organisations remain for less time in each job, the scope for movement by others would be greater. But there is still a danger that job moves around a very large entity - such as a Shell or a Unilever - may not be enough to change the culture.

Unilever, for example, takes pride in having an enlightened policy for moving its most promising managers between quite different posts, although still within Unilever. So, for example, a production manager may become a transport manager, a finance manager a factory manager, and so on. But even the most enthusiastic policy for moving managers round large companies will not expose them to radically different cultures. Large businesses deliberately seek to make their cultures all-pervasive. Hence, a manager moved to another part of the same firm in a different country, will often find the same all-pervading culture.

To change cultures requires new questioning, even iconoclasm. It means encouraging movement between organisations, not simply within them, and therefore calls for long-term career moves rather than short-term exchanges.

For many years, the difficulty of transferring pension rights between organisations was a big obstacle. Over the last quarter century or so, progress has been made. Yet both within the private sector, and especially between the public and private sectors, more needs to be done to assist mobility through making pension arrangements more readily transferable.

Moving in and out of the public sector

The main concern with the public sector is a much bigger one. Top civil servants do not stay in their jobs too long; they stay in the public sector too long. The veritable gulf which still exists between the public and private sectors, and their cultures, needs to be bridged. As Section 4 showed, there are bound to be some differences between these cultures, but there need not and should not be a gulf. How can movement between the two sectors help to reduce it?

For many years, some people have moved between the two sectors but these exchanges have had little effect. Neither side has been prepared to send its best people and the exchanges do not last long - only, say, two years.

Those who moved into the public sector have therefore not been taken seriously. They were, anyway, boarders to be repelled. In addition, few incomers worked at a high enough level to bring about real change. Perhaps the most important exceptions were the businessmen like John Hoskyns, Derek Rayner, David Young and Robin Ibbs who Mrs Thatcher brought in, and who did have a significant impact. Even so, that impact was less permanent than it might have been because they were not succeeded by outsiders of similar calibre and drive.

In conclusion then, cultural change in the civil service depends on the movement of more and abler people from outside the service, for longer periods (five years instead of two) and into more senior positions. Above all, it requires people with an ability to act as effective, persuasive, change agents and not simply as conventional administrators or professionals.

Training the elite

There must also be parallel moves out of the public sector. The conventional wisdom is that only France has substantial and fruitful two-way movement between the highest levels of business and government. It is said that a major reason for this is that those concerned have shared high-level technical and administrative education and training at elite 'grandes écoles.' The UK does not possess a range and quality of high-level academic schools like those in France, but my own attempt to move us minimally in this direction in the 1960s perhaps provides a lesson.

I was, at that stage, a member of the Osmond Committee set up in Whitehall to recommend ways of improving management training in the civil service. Its conclusions were assimilated into the (1970) Fulton report on the Civil Service.[20] The most significant outcome of this was the establishment of the Civil Service College, but I tried, as I believed, to improve on this.

I pointed out that the UK had recently established two major business schools (London and Manchester), one of whose weak spots was that few civil servants attended. I therefore suggested that instead of seeking the establishment of a civil service college we should instead recommend the establishment of a third Business School. This would be on the understanding that about one third of those attending the masters' degree programmes at each of the three schools would in future come from the civil service.

The proposal was rejected, mainly because one of the civil service trade unions, whose secretary was a member of the Committee, was determined to see a wholly separate institution established for the Civil Service. We shall never know what my proposal would have achieved. But I still insist that mixing, over the last 20 years, some

4,000 bright young business people with some 2,000 bright young civil servants could not have avoided improving relations between government and business in the UK - quite apart from what the training itself would have achieved.

It follows that, in addition to making determined efforts to move bright people between the higher levels of the civil service and other organisations in Britain, the country really does need to look again at this issue. We need ways of ensuring that promising young people work together - not separately - during their formative years by being trained together.

Schools

Finally, what about education? I have pointed to two consequences of the fact that virtually no school teacher has worked for long outside the educational system. First, they have little understanding of the thinking and skills currently needed in the real world, let alone those that will be needed in the 21st century. Second, they do not understand how businesses operate and, in particular, the emphasis they put on team work. Schools continue to over-emphasise the performance of children as individuals, not their ability to work successfully and creatively in teams.

In an ideal world, one would insist that teachers moved between jobs in education and elsewhere several times during a career. Although that is an unreachable target, we should insist that every teacher should work in one or two, not more, non-school, preferably private sector, jobs before the age of 40, ideally during their early 30s. The period outside should be not less than two years. Nor is there any reason why lecturers in further education colleges should be treated differently. Lecturers engaged in teacher training should move for similar spells into the classroom.

Universities

The position in universities is more complicated. University teachers need to move out into the real world at least as much as school teachers. Over-specialisation might, however, make useful moves difficult to arrange, and many academics would drive real-world employers to distraction.

What should take place in universities is therefore what should happen in any case. They must become more open, with a substantial increase in the number of educational and training programmes run for adults, and the use of more well-qualified people to contribute as speakers or tutors.

If this does not occur, the demise of the traditional university will be hastened. Increasingly, people outside universities will be working in similar ways and with similar education and talents. They will do so more innovatively and with greater vigour because they will be untrammelled by academic traditions and preconceptions. They will be able to compete with universities and, increasingly, they will do so. This will be a powerful form of coercion which will force abandonment of the pretence that only a university faculty, pinned in its ghetto, is capable of running a university. The new republic of the intellect will have arrived.

Those who believe that universities cannot meet this challenge should think again. A recent study by university trade unions shows that more than half of all university staff will retire within the next 20 years. We should not bemoan this but rather grasp it as a heaven-sent opportunity to make a dramatic break with the past. We should bring in people who have worked for substantial periods outside universities and make full use of information and communications technology, in part as a substitute for people. My objectives can, if we wish it, be achieved more easily in universities than in any other sector. But if they do prove more difficult to achieve, what then? Section 6 tackles this issue.

6 THE NEED FOR ORGANISATIONAL BIRTH AND DEATH

a) The Private Sector

The most radical way of changing cultures is through the birth or death of whole organisations - by introducing quite new cultures or killing off old ones. The idea of organisational death is seen as so radical that it is widely resisted, even by people unconnected with the organisation under threat. Birth is easier.

By far the biggest proportion of new organisations being created in the UK are businesses and, by definition, they establish distinctive cultures deriving from the founding individual or team. The large-scale creation of new businesses keeps economies flexible. This can be seen most clearly in the 'Pacific Tigers' - Hong Kong, Singapore, Taiwan and South Korea. There, the birth of new companies with new cultures has been the driving force behind the most rapid economic expansion anywhere, in the whole of human history.[21]

Since about 1980, conditions have been especially favourable to an increase in the number of new businesses in the UK. The current age, which sociologists have dubbed 'post-industrial,' is not one where industry has disappeared. It is one where the large, labour-intensive manufacturing plants of the 1960s - the Longbridges and Cowleys - have been replaced by plants where employment, but not necessarily output, has fallen.

In this respect the enterprise society of the 1980s was not a political gimmick. It was brought into being by underlying forces. These were partly technical, for example computer systems which made greater automation in manufacturing possible. They were partly the result of the development of knowledge businesses - engaged in design, marketing, financial and other advice, consultancy and training.[22] In an era when they are an engine of economic growth, the main role of policy makers in government is to put as few obstacles as possible in the way of the birth and growth of new businesses, something which Brussels, and perhaps Whitehall, bureaucrats do not yet understand.

b) The Public Sector

We have seen that the public sector contains the main obstacles to the changing of cultures by the death - and perhaps surprisingly the birth - of organisations. Birth will be difficult because public expenditure in the UK is bound to be constrained for the rest of the century at a time when we know that transfer payments such as pensions are bound to increase. The scope for establishing new public sector bodies is therefore bound to be limited.

There is, however, an impression of change. In 1992 the Duke of Edinburgh's Commonwealth Study Conference brought some 250 of the most promising future leaders of the Commonwealth to the UK, and divided them into groups of about 15, each of which visited a different part of the UK. Many of these groups commented critically on the confusing multiplicity of schemes aimed at regional development or urban regeneration, using various grants and tax concessions. One group spoke of 'initiative fever.' With initiative piled on initiative the public sector has succeeded in giving a greater impression of dynamism than is justified. The rest of us may feel that we are eavesdropping not on the birth of genuinely new organisations, but on an endless rejuggling of acronyms.

This makes it important for the public sector to do what it can to generate movement within the sector by closing organisations down. One sentence in Donald Schon's 1970 Reith Lectures has remained with me over the years: 'In government, as in most other established institutions,' he wrote, 'the organisational equivalent of biological death is missing.'[23]

It is important that we should take what opportunities there are to kill off parts of the public sector that are no longer useful. In the USA, for example, the disbanding of an agency is 'an event frequently discussed, but almost never undertaken.'[24] Yet there are many ways in which organisational death could be arranged.

*   Privatisation. Privatisation does not mean closure, but it does mean shaking off the civil service culture. This can be difficult, especially in large organisations such as British Telecom where cultural change is taking much time and effort.

We have already noted the rise of British Gas in public esteem. This pre-dates privatisation, although the brilliant 'Tell Sid!' campaign launched to solicit subscriptions to British Gas's shares made the organisation seem more human. The change in British Gas has been a result of careful and sustained internal effort.

The change in British Airways' culture, ably sponsored by Sir Colin Marshall, was similarly the result of hard and persistent work, although the recent charges by Virgin of 'dirty tricks' have undermined some of BA's success. This demonstrates, among other things, that the culture of an organisation is indivisible.

Privatisation has also removed another aspect of the civil service culture. So long as an industry is in the public sector its sponsoring government department is extremely reluctant to stop monitoring it, and in differing degrees interfering with it. As everyone knew, and as privatisation has shown, it was unnecessary to have large numbers of officials in a sponsoring department monitoring the industry, while a similar number of people within the industry were employed to monitor the monitors, and respond where necessary. Much of the monitoring was niggling. Being overseen in this way simply reinforced the civil service culture within the nationalised industry. It was the wrong sort of contagion.

* Project Organisations. Whenever a new public sector body is established - and indeed for ones which already exist - those responsible for its establishment should, if possible, plan to disband it once its task has been completed. The strength of the desire to do the opposite is shown by the fact that, even in the rather rare cases where a body is set up to perform a particular task, it will look for ways to continue once the task is completed.

An outstanding example is the National Aeronautics and Space Agency (NASA) which was set up in the USA to carry out the space programme and to put men on the moon. Once it was clear that the moon programme was over, NASA exerted strong pressure for it to be given a major new task, for example to revitalise American cities. NASA's employees did not want the personal and professional upheaval which they would otherwise face. In the event, no alternative to the moon programme was established.

In this country, we should have begun much sooner to explore the use of project organisations. Having failed to do so, we should now establish the principle that wherever possible, public bodies should be given a clearly defined task to carry out. Once it is completed they should be closed.

* Time-limited organisations. Indeed, we should go

further and establish the principle that, after a specified period of time, all public sector bodies will be examined on the assumption that they will be closed unless they can show good reason for continuing. This does happen within some public bodies, although it is not a regular practice with whole organisations.

For example, the Economic and Social Research Council strongly - and to my surprise - insisted in 1987 that the Council's Designated Research Centres, which financed smallish teams of researchers in selected universities, would cease to be given further grants after ten years. Why should similar procedures not be accepted more generally - and for complete organisations?

* Branches. Where a large organisation like the National Health Service or the state school system has many relatively small units, there will often be pressure to close some of them. For example, a local population may have declined relative to other areas. In all cases there will be strong resistance to any change. The recent furore over the London teaching hospitals, and the successful campaign against the proposed merger of Birkbeck College and University College London in 1986/7 are just two examples. Whatever the merits of the case, it is fairly easy to orchestrate a media campaign against change.

The obvious answer is an enquiry into a closure proposal - with evidence from all concerned. The problem is that any enquiry will probably be conducted by peers. They will find a genuinely independent judgement difficult. They will either not want to damage a friendly institution, if only because they may fear weakening their own positions if their institutions come under similar pressure in future. Alternatively, if they are enemies, they may welcome an opportunity to undermine it.

Even so, given that change in the public sector culture is

so difficult, it is important that none of the few genuine opportunities for change through closure should be missed. Technology will provide some of these. For example, given that universities need to be far more innovative in their use of information and communications technology, there is a case for closing some of the lowest ranking ones now and replacing them with a second (and even a third) open university.

* Fossilisation. The most difficult choices arise where an organisation's culture no longer leaves it fully fit. Unfortunately, no organisation will itself admit that it has ceased to fulfil its purpose while outsiders, lacking information, will find it difficult to prove.

Most of us will have candidates for closure, perhaps followed by later rebirth, in the private sector. The Jockey Club, the MCC and the Football League would be high on most peoples' lists. The argument for such toughness must be that the organisation is so inappropriate to the present era that even if it is still needed, it should start afresh. Beginning with an entirely new set of people may be the only way out.

Given that it may be difficult to judge from the outside whether a body is outmoded there is a case in some fields for adopting a rota system for closure. This would be especially appropriate with universities. No one who has visited a university or department where most of the staff have been in the same place for 20 years or more could be happy with the weary cynicism and lethargy which now infect it.

On the same basis, I have at intervals suggested that one or two Oxford or Cambridge colleges should be closed each year, at least over the next two decades. Each could be allowed to restart after three years, on the understanding that no one who had ever taught in either university could join the resurrected college. Just imagine the media campaign which would follow that!

Many people have other candidates in the public sector for radical change, the Foreign Office and the Treasury being high on the list. With large bodies like this, the suggestion of closure would be treated as proof of lunacy. That does, however, reinforce the case for contagion. Substantial transfers of people should take place, especially at the top of the organisation. There is even a case for looking at whether, over a period, these august institutions should replace their entire staff by rota.

7 OPENNESS

To some degree the proposals in Sections 5 and 6 are defeatist. They assume that in this country we shall find it so difficult to develop learning organisations that coercion and contagion will have to play a big part in allowing us to escape our culture trap.

Whether I am right in this, or whether coaching or their own actions will enable organisations successfully to change their cultures, the message with which we must end is about openness and about porousness. Contagion from outside, which is an important second best to internal learning, cannot change a closed culture because the culture does not let it in. We must take the need to create more movement between organisations and sectors very seriously, as we must the need for time limits on jobs. Five years in the job, ten years in the organisation, should be the slogan.

Movement, whether between organisations or between jobs, creates both a need to learn and an opportunity for the individual to do so. A new role brings new opportunities, new challenges and new perspectives. It also takes the holder of that role at least the first part of the way towards joining with others to create a learning organisation.

Killing off an entity altogether is, of course, more painful, because it affects more people and does so more traumatically. Yet, by the same token, it creates the possibility for more learning, through retraining for example.

And where an entity succeeds in changing itself, whether through coaching or not, openness will have played an important role. An organisation must have openness to the coach; to ideas about change and how to achieve it, whether these come from inside or outside the organisation; to dialogue within the organisation and between those engaged in the dialogue, their coaches and the outside world. Only an open organisation can work out how to learn, how the outside world is changing and how the organisation itself should therefore respond.

Openness is the key to successful change, including successful cultural change. There is no aphorism which says that an organisation closed in upon itself cannot succeed. But there should be.

APPENDIX: ORGANISATIONAL LEARNING

If learning is the most elusive, and perhaps the most important mechanism for cultural change in the years ahead, what are its features?

Three components are essential:

Visionary thinking - The first is an ability to generate a common purpose, using the organisation's values to create broad visions of its future which those who work in it will accept. This will make it possible to set precise objectives and goals for performance in the entity's market place, whether that is commercial or social (and if it is a public body it is essential that inputs are not regarded as proxies for measuring outputs). The establishment of such goals for the organisation will then lead on to views about the resources - people, money, equipment etc - which it needs to achieve them, as well as a structure that can do so. Becoming a learning organisation is first of all, then, a matter of vision.

Dialogue - The more the process of working out acceptable values, vision, goals and structures enables an organisation to create common expectations for all who work in it, the more it will create a common purpose. That is why the second feature of a learning organisation is dialogue. Without it, even if a common purpose has been agreed, it is unlikely to be sustained.

In today's complex and changing world, values, vision, goals, strategy and structure have to be kept up to date and in line. To do this, now that organisations employ substantial numbers of intelligent and often argumentative people, means that it is increasingly important to organise purposeful conversation - perhaps dialogue is the better word - at every level in the organisation. And this dialogue must create learning teams. They must not only seek steady improvement in organisational structures and operational performance. They must continually bring those who join in the dialogue back to the organisation's values and culture, ensuring that these inform its thinking and behaviour.

A key point here is that an effective organisational structure - again whether in a commercial organisation or not - must be able to deal both with the 'inside and now' - to make certain that current activities are performed well - and with the 'outside and the future' - to ensure that the organisation will survive into that future.[25] If too few resources are devoted to either of these activities, the entity will find it difficult to remain viable, let alone to succeed. Either it will not learn how to satisfy present clients, owners or employees, or it will not find profitable and worthwhile ways of doing so in the future.

Systems thinking - The third prerequisite of a learning organisation is systems thinking. This is also now a prerequisite for any kind of organisational leadership. One reason why so many British organisations are currently trapped by their cultures is that this is inadequately recognised.[26]

A system is a set of elements which relate to each other in a coherent way; without coherence this would not be a system, only chaos. We are all used to the idea of a railway system or a road system. Managers talk of a production system or an information system. Systems thinking requires us to recognise that the firm as a whole - including its financial, technical, human and other elements - is itself a complex socio-technical system. This is why systems thinking must represent an important attribute of the learning organisation.

Timing

A salutary point must be made here. This is that success can make it almost more difficult for an organisation to change than failure. Past achievement too often means that the traditions which made that achievement possible have become so ingrained that they are impossible to alter. Twenty years afterwards, I have never forgotten the words of the then chairman of the University Grants Committee to the top echelon of an institution experiencing world acclaim: 'Things are fine now, but in twenty years everything will be set in concrete.'

There is always a problem of timing if an organisation is to change before that concrete has set. Well-established institutions suffer from the oil-tanker syndrome, as is exemplified by recent events at Lloyds. The momentum continues apparently unchecked, well after things have started to go wrong. By the time it is clear that they have gone wrong, the established culture is so out of date that only radical reform will do. With Lloyds, the problem was not simply that £3bn was lost in 1990. The fundamental question was whether the established culture, with its assumption that wealthy private individuals could continue to finance all risks in a rapidly changing world, remained appropriate.

SUMMARY

There is widespread concern about our national culture, or rather the individual cultures of the organisations, grand or common place, which make it up.

1 CULTURES

The culture of an organisation reflects how those in it think and act: it shows 'how we do things here.' An inappropriate organisational culture can be changed in four ways. These are **coercion**: e.g. competition or take-over; **contagion**: where individuals or groups from outside bring in a new culture; **coaching**: where an organisation brings in outside experts to help it change; and **learning**, where the organisation itself learns how to adapt. This is the best way to change a culture. It requires the creation of a 'learning organisation.'

2 PUBLIC AND PRIVATE SECTOR CULTURES

a) Private Sector

Change is continuously forced on private-sector organisations through: changes in their environment, especially markets; failure to achieve profit targets, resulting in pressure from shareholders and the financial press; the threat of take-over, which often leads to improved performance and actual take-over, which often guarantees it. During periods like the recent recession, the pressure for change is general. Global markets mean that change today is very rapid, keeping organisations awake and alert. But several concerns remain.

i) The best guarantee that competition remains adequate is an active government competition policy. But politicians still have too much discretion over whether to accept Monopolies and Mergers Commission findings.

ii) Top executives' pay has risen rapidly and there has been an impression that financial rewards are greater if top executives fail than if they succeed.

iii) The framework for corporate governance has not provided appropriate disciplines. The Cadbury Committee has suggested improvements, but many doubt whether this self-regulatory approach will be sufficient to prevent more direct government interference.

iv) Some chairmen and chief executives remain too long at the top of private sector organisations. The concern over directorships is even greater. Many board members - executive or non-executive - serve for more than 20 years.

b) Public Sector

Public organisations can pursue broader objectives than profit-making businesses. But it is more difficult for them to abandon activities. Perhaps surprisingly, those in top public sector jobs seem to move more frequently between jobs than they would in the private sector. But there are concerns over the public sector too.

i) Schools

Given the need for 'learning organisations,' it is worrying that the cultures of schools put too little emphasis on learning as opposed to teaching. There is too little overlap between the cultures of schools and of the world outside, especially since teachers hold that they, not outsiders, know what should be taught. Nor does the culture of the civil service help. The culture of the Department of Education has not come to terms with the information and communications revolution. Its attempt to introduce testing of the national curriculum has imposed excessive form-filling on teachers. These failings suggest that the school system and the assumptions which underlie it are now part of the problem, not the solution.

ii) Universities

Universities are too isolated from the outside world and have not recognised what information and communication technologies will demand of them by the 21st century. Like schools, they concentrate too narrowly on the performance of students as individuals, not as members of teams. They put teaching ahead of learning. They largely ignore specialists and professionals outside universities, often their former students, who would welcome help from universities with their professional development and could offer help in return. Research findings are too often kept within small, closed communities of scholars. Findings are rarely written clearly and simply enough to make them generally available. There is too much emphasis on evaluation of research by peers in narrow disciplines. Often there must be doubt about whether a conventional university degree offers a good basis for working in a non-university job.

iii) Civil service

The core civil service's main role is now in policy work and in supervising devolved agencies. The emphasis is moving away from the traditional bureaucracy, which was at its best in establishing procedures, setting rules and applying them rigorously. But the civil service under-rates its deficiencies in tackling strategy and policy. The most important are the following: policy work requires vision and imagination and these are not traditional civil service qualities; the civil service culture is predominantly a literary one, unable to make sense of the complex socio-technical systems of the modern world; civil service policy thinking is too solitary and civil servants find it difficult to construct and operate in multi-disciplinary teams. To ensure that rules were kept, the traditional civil service actually enforced a non-learning culture.

iv) Government agencies

The creation of government agencies makes it possible for them to be increasingly freed from detailed central control. They can now develop their own cultures. The problems of changing culture, and especially of learning to be more effective are, however, inadequately understood.

v) Principles for change

- Changing cultures depends on bringing new questioning, even iconoclasm, into them. A newcomer is more likely to make the naive or unconventional challenge and to notice previously unrecognised patterns which lead to advance.

- Movement, whether between organisations or jobs, requires that individuals learn. It brings new opportunities, challenges and perspectives.

- The development of a culture in which both generalists and specialists, throughout the public and private sectors, move more freely between jobs and thereby learn more about both jobs and organisations, can only be beneficial for Britain.

- There is a need to institute more purposeful conversations, perhaps a better word is dialogue, at all levels in the organisation, and between those levels too.

3   RECOMMENDATIONS

Jobs - No-one in the top two or three tiers of any major organisation should remain in the same job for more than five years.

- There should be strong, independent non-executive directors on all company boards. They should be given initial appointments of two years, followed by further appointments up to a maximum of six years.

- There is no reason to exempt specialists, such as scientists, engineers or accountants, from these recommendations.

Organisations - Movement should be encouraged between organisations, not simply within them, through long-term career moves and not short-term exchanges.

- The principle should be: five years in the job; ten years in the organisation.

- There is a particular need for the exchange between the public and private sectors of substantial numbers of able people for significant periods, for example, four or five years.

- Ways should be found to enable promising young people from the public and private sectors to work together during training.

Schools - School teachers should work in one or two non-school jobs before the age of 40, and preferably during their early 30s. Lecturers in further education colleges should not be exempt from this.

Universities - The fact that about half of all university staff will retire within 20 years should be grasped as a heaven sent opportunity. It will enable people from outside universities to be brought in, and will ensure full use of information and communications technology, in part as a substitute for people.

- To ensure that enough students in higher education are usefully trained for real-world jobs, about half of our universities should be reconverted to polytechnics.

Organisational birth and death

Apart from privatisation, which can have beneficial effects in changing cultures, other means should be used.

- Wherever possible, new public sector bodies should be established as project organisations, with clearly defined tasks. Once the tasks are completed, the organisations should be closed.

- Even where a project cannot be identified in this way, public-sector organisations should be time-limited. After a specified period, they should be examined on the assumption that they will be closed unless there is good reason for continuing.

- Large state organisations, like the National Health Service, the state school system or the universities, which contain large numbers of institutions, should not be reluctant to close some of them where this is justified.

- The public and private sectors in general should be tougher in closing organisations which have become inappropriate. If the organisation is still needed, it can begin afresh, with entirely new people.

NOTES

1. For a stimulating but idiosyncratic introduction to organisational cultures, see Charles Handy, *Gods of Management*, Pan Books, London, 1985.

2 I know how difficult the position of a newcomer can be. I was asked by Jeremy Bray to join the North Western Gas Board in the 1960s to try to push them more quickly into using modern management techniques and methods - a thankless task, since I was greatly outnumbered.

3 See Peter M Senge, *The Fifth Discipline*, Century Business, London, 1992, especially chapter 1. Inevitably, because it is a new concept, there is much dispute over precisely what a learning organisation can learn and how. This book gives a good, mainstream account of what a learning organisation is and does. Chapter 1 sets out the basic concepts, which are explored and applied in the remainder of the volume, although the systems model is very simplistic when compared with that of Stafford Beer, see note 5.

4 *Report of the Committee on the Financial Aspects of Corporate Governance*, Gee, London, 1992

5. These figures come from a survey of the top 50 companies carried out for Demos by Duncan McKechnie in July 1993.

6 See Stafford Beer, *The Heart of Enterprise*, Wiley, Chichester, UK, 1979, chapters 2 to 4. References numbered 23 and 24 should be taken with this one. *The Heart of Enterprise* is essential reading for anyone who wishes to understand how complex systems, especially businesses and other organisations, can remain viable. As the passage referred to in note 24 explains, those who lead organisations do so best if they can master the art of systems thinking. Beer's book provides what is, in my view, the most helpful basis there is for that. It is a weighty volume in all senses of the word, but will repay careful study by those who persist.

Stafford Beer begins with an explanation of what a system is (Chapter 1) and proceeds to set out the essential characteristics

(Chapter 1) and proceeds to set out the essential characteristics which a system must have if it is to be viable in chapters 2 to 4.

The notion of variety reduction, which is the subject of this note, is another very useful concept for managers and one which is inadequately understood and used.

7 Howard Gardner, *Frames of Mind*, Fontana Press, London, 1993. See especially chapter 13.

8 From an unpublished proposal to the Department for Education from Education 2000, February 1993. The Education 2000 Trust is based at Letchworth Garden City, Hertfordshire, UK.

9 Howard Gardner, *The Unschooled Mind*, Fontana Press, London, 1993. See especially, chapter 13.

10 Sir Douglas Hague, *Beyond Universities*, Hobart Paper 115, Institute of Economic Affairs, London, 1991.

11 Peter Drucker, *Sunday Times*, May 30, 1993.

12 Michael Dixon, *Financial Times*, March 17, 1993.

13 See Gareth Morgan, *Images of Organisation*, Sage Publications, Beverly Hills, California, USA, 1986. In a remarkable book, which has received wide acclaim, Gareth Morgan has pulled together virtually all that matters in recent writings on organisation theory in an imaginative and practical way. He believes that good managers and professionals become skilled at 'reading' the situations they have to handle and this book seeks to make such a skill accessible to the rest of us. The author uses a series of metaphors - or images - each of which throws light on the characteristics of a particular type of organisation or a particular aspect of a number of organisations. The images use familiar notions so that organisations can be likened to machines, organisms, brains, political systems, psychic prisons, instruments of domination etc. Chapter 2 which considers the organisation as a machine therefore looks at bureaucracies, like the civil service and

should be read in that context. Readers will also find useful chapter 4, on organisations as brains, chapter 5, as cultures, etc. Anyone interested in obtaining a splendid insight into this field is encouraged to read the whole book. A more recent publication by the same author is *Imaginization*, Sage Publications, London, 1993. It will not appeal to everyone, being laced with somewhat humorous illustrations to make it more accessible. Charts like that on p. 95 are, however, helpful in showing how Morgan's metaphors can be used to analyse real-world problems.

14 I hasten to make my peace with those government departments which do use mathematics and diagrams. I think especially of the Treasury, whose large model of the UK economy is used extensively and well, despite jibes to the contrary from outside. I would, however, make two points. First, the Treasury is unusual among civil service departments in being so non-literary. Second, even the Treasury model follows standard macro-economic practice in using monetary amounts to report on very complex socio/technical/economic phenomena. GDP is a good example. This does not 'make sense' of complex systems but avoids the problem of doing so by reducing them to sums of money, as all macro-economics does. It is variety reduction of a very high order.

15 I have myself argued that 'however academic and business thinking on managerial issues changes, the civil service machine goes on operating in time-honoured ways. It does so because civil servants spend too little of their time thinking and learning about organisational processes and because those who do think about them are rarely promoted to the interesting or glamorous positions in the service.' This is taken from 'Can Scientists Manage Science?' in Douglas Hague, editor, *The Management of Science*, Macmillan, Basingstoke and London, 1991.

16 *Improving Management in Government: The Next Steps*, Report to the Prime Minister, HM Stationery Office, London, 1988. All passages quoted in Section 4 (c) are from this Report.

17 For example, in the first corporate plan of the Economic and Social Research Council, written under my Chairmanship, we expressed our wish 'to discourage the mentality of an unquestioned research-career-for-life' and 'to avoid...the support of intellectual establishments which are living on past reputation and no longer deliver.' Economic and Social Research Council, *Corporate Plan, 1986-1991*, ESRC, Swindon, UK, 1986.

18 James D Watson, *The Double Helix*, Weidenfeld and Nicholson, London,1968, gives a full account of this discovery and, even so long after the event, is as gripping as many whodunnits. Francis Crick, *What Mad Pursuit?*, Weidenfeld and Nicholson, London, 1988 gives a shorter account, in Crick's lively style. It also shows how he has applied the lessons of his discoveries in other fields, both inside and outside science.

19 Peter Hennessy, unpublished lecture to an Educational Innovation Conference, Templeton College, Oxford, July, 1990.

20 The Civil Service, *Report of the Fulton Committee, 1966-68*, Command Paper 3638, HM Stationery Office, London, 1968.

21 See, for example, John Naisbitt and Patricia Aburdene, *Mega-Trends 2000*, Sidgwick & Jackson, 1988, chapter 6.

22 Sir Douglas Hague, *Beyond Universities*, quoted above. See especially chapter 4 which gives a brief survey of the nature and role of knowledge industries.

23 Donald A Schon, *Beyond the Stable State*, Random House, New York, USA, p. 163. Although now somewhat dated, this is a pithy and well-written account of the kind of issue - e.g. organisational conservatism and learning - dealt with in this paper. Chapter 5, on 'Government as a learning system' raises important issues in a transatlantic context.

24 *Ibid*, p.175.

25 See Stafford Beer, *op. cit.* Among the most crucial elements in an organisation are, or should be, the sub-systems which monitor and respond to what is going on within the organisation (the inside and now) and what externally (the outside and then). Chapters 8 and 9 explain this.

26 See Stafford Beer, cited above, chapter 1. One of Stafford Beer's concerns is that too often we fail to look at a large enough system when faced with managerial or political problems. Readers could usefully ponder the implications of and the lessons that can be learned from his assertion (p. 90) that because the sub-system we have traditionally considered is too small 'the penal system becomes a training machine for felons.'

Demos

Demos is an independent think-tank set up to improve the breadth and quality of political and policy debate. It encourages radical thinking and solutions to the long-term problems facing the UK and other advanced industrial societies. It brings together thinkers and doers.

Demos is a registered charity. It is financed by voluntary donations from individuals, foundations and companies.

The views expressed in publications are those of the authors alone. They do not represent Demos' institutional viewpoint.

If you wish to receive all of Demos' pamphlets, you can become a subscriber.

For £40 for individuals, and £80 for organisations, you will receive:

* a minimum of 8 pamphlets of policy, argument and analysis
* a newsletter of ideas and events
* access to conferences, dinners and events

_____

I want to become a Demos subscriber and I enclose a cheque for £40/£25 for student-unwaged-OAP/£80 for institutions (delete as necessary), made out to 'Demos,' for a year's subscription:

Name:..

Address: ....

.... tel: ....

Institution/position:..

Areas of interest: ....

Please send me further information about making a donation to Demos ___ (tick)

Please post as soon as possible to Demos: 120 Wilton Road, London SW1V 1GZ

Other Demos publications available for £5.95 post free from Demos, 120 Wilton Rd, London SW1V 1GZ.

Reconnecting Taxation   by Geoff Mulgan and Robin Murray

Over the last 200 years our tax and spending systems have been repeatedly revolutionised. Today we are on the brink of another revolution. A far-reaching new wave of reform is now needed to bring tax structures into line with the realities of a global economy and the values of less deferential and more democratic consumer societies. In an age when citizens are no longer prepared to write blank cheques for government, Mulgan and Murray make the case for reconnecting the taxes people pay to the services they receive.

Geoff Mulgan is Director of Demos. Robin Murray is a Fellow of the Institute of Development Studies at Sussex University. According to the _Financial Times_, the pamphlet 'provokes exactly the sort of longer-term thinking which is missing from the current political debate.'

An End to Illusions   by Alan Duncan

In the late 1980s political leaders claimed that Britain was experiencing an economic miracle. The years of decline had come to an end. Instead the 1990s began with unprecedented debt, a deep recession and a credit squeeze that destroyed thousands of businesses and caused hundreds of thousands of repossessions. Duncan argues that unless the UK's financial institutions, housing and investment policy are radically reformed the illusions and mistakes will simply be repeated. He calls for the demerger of the clearing banks, the ending of mortgage subsidies and independence for the Bank of England.

Alan Duncan is Conservative MP for Rutland and Mellon.

He entered the House of Commons in 1992. According to George Walden writing in the _Daily Telegraph_ the pamphlet 'provides three things in scant supply: a disinterested assessment of what went wrong with the British economic miracle in the 1980s; thoughts on how we can avoid making the same mistakes again, and a lucid style to expound his ideas.'